CROCHET
8-Hour Fashion Scarves™

Designs by Mickie Akins

General Information

Many of the products used in this pattern book can be purchased from local craft, fabric and variety stores, or from the Annie's Attic Needlecraft Catalog *(see Customer Service information on page 15).*

Contents

SKILL LEVEL

INTERMEDIATE

FINISHED SIZE

3 x 56 inches, excluding Fringe

MATERIALS

- Patons Grace light (light worsted) weight yarn (1¾ oz/136 yds/50g per ball): 1 ball #60902 spearmint
- Size D/3/3.25mm crochet hook or size needed to obtain gauge

GAUGE

5 sc = 1 inch; 6 rows = 2 inches

SPECIAL STITCHES

V-stitch (V-st): (Tr, ch 1, tr) in next st.

Decrease (dec): Holding back last lp of each st on hook, tr in next st, sk next st, tr in next st, yo, pull through all lps on hook.

INSTRUCTIONS

SCARF

Row 1: Ch 282, sc in **back bar** (see Fig 1.) of 2nd ch from hook and in each ch across, turn. *(281 sc)*

Fig. 1
Back Bar of Chain

Row 2: Ch 4 *(counts as first tr)*, sk next st, **V-st** *(see Special Stitches)* in next st, [sk next 2 sts, V-st in next st] across to last 2 sts, sk next st, tr in last st, turn. *(93 V-sts, 2 tr)*

Row 3: Ch 2 *(counts as first hdc)*, hdc in each st and in each ch across, turn.

Row 4: Ch 4 *(counts as first tr and ch-2)*, [**dec** *(see Special Stitches)*, ch 2] across to last st, tr in last st, turn.

Row 5: Ch 2, hdc in each st and in each ch across, turn.

Rows 6–9: Rep rows 2–5 consecutively. At end of last row, fasten off.

Fringe

Cut 2 strands each 12 inches in length. Holding both strands tog, fold in half. Pull fold through, pull ends through fold. Pull to tighten.

Add fringe to end of each row on each short end of Scarf. ❑❑

Mulberry Scarf

SKILL LEVEL

INTERMEDIATE

FINISHED SIZE

3¾ x 63½ inches, excluding Fringe

MATERIALS

- ❑ Red Heart LusterSheen fine (sport) weight yarn (4 oz/335 yds/113g per skein): 1 skein each #0518 light mulberry, #0519 dark mulberry and #0805 natural
- ❑ Size D/3/3.25mm crochet hook or size needed to obtain gauge

FINE

GAUGE

6 dc = 1¼ inches; 7 rows = 2 inches

PATTERN NOTES

Leave 5-inch end at beginning and end of each row to be included in Fringe.

Do not turn, unless otherwise stated.

SPECIAL STITCH

V-stitch (V-st): (Dc, ch 1, dc) in next st.

INSTRUCTIONS

SCARF

Row 1: With dark mulberry *(see Pattern Notes)*, ch 307, dc in **back bar** *(see Fig. 1)* of 4th ch from hook and in back bar each ch across, **do not turn** *(see Pattern Notes)*. Fasten off. *(305 dc)*

Fig. 1
Back Bar of Chain

Row 2: Join light mulberry with sl st in first st, ch 4 *(counts as first dc and ch-1)*, sk next st, [**V-st** *(see Special Stitch)* in next st, sk next st] across to last st, dc in last st. Fasten off. *(2 dc, 151 V-sts)*

Row 3: Join natural with sc in first st, sc in each st and in each ch across. Fasten off. *(456 sc)*

Row 4: Join dark mulberry with sl st in first st, ch 4, sk next st, [V-st in next st, sk next 2 sts] across with dc in last st. Fasten off. *(2 dc, 151 V-sts)*

Row 5: Join light mulberry with sl st, ch 3, sk next st, [V-st in next ch sp] across with dc in last st.

Row 6: Join natural with sl st in first st, ch 3, dc in each st and in each ch across. Fasten off. *(455 dc)*

Row 7: Join dark mulberry with sc in first st, ch 1, sk next st, [sc in next st, ch 2, sk next 2 sts] across to last 3 sts, sc in next st, ch 1, sk next st, sc in last st. Fasten off.

Rows 8–13: Working in starting ch on opposite side of row 1, rep rows 2–7.

Fringe

Cut 1 strand of each color 10 inches in length. Fold strands in half, pull fold through, pull all ends through fold. Pull tight.

Add fringe to end of each row on each short end of Scarf. ❑❑

Light Green Scarf

SKILL LEVEL

INTERMEDIATE

FINISHED SIZE

3½ x 55½ inches, excluding Fringe

MATERIALS

❑ Red Heart LusterSheen fine (sport) weight yarn (4 oz/335 yds/113g per skein): 1 skein #0615 tea leaf
❑ Size D/3/3.25mm crochet hook or size needed to obtain gauge

GAUGE

13 sc = 2 inches; 7 rows = 2 inches

INSTRUCTIONS

SCARF

Row 1: Ch 362, sc in **back bar** (see Fig. 1) of 2nd ch from hook and in each ch across, turn. (361 sc)

Fig. 1
Back Bar of Chain

Row 2: Ch 1, sc in first st, [ch 5, sk next 2 sts, sc in next st] across to last 3 sts, ch 2, sk next 2 sts, dc in last st forming last ch sp, turn. (120 ch sps)

Row 3: Ch 5 (counts as first dc and ch-2), dc in 3rd ch of next ch-5 sp, ch 2, **dc dec** (see Stitch Guide) in last ch worked in and 3rd ch of next ch sp, [ch 2, dc dec in last ch worked in and 3rd ch of next ch sp] across, ch 2, tr in last st, turn.

Row 4: Ch 1, sc in each st and in each ch across, turn. (361 sc)

Rows 5–13: [Rep rows 2–4 consecutively] 3 times. At end of last row, fasten off.

Fringe

Cut 2 strands each 18 inches long. Holding both strands tog, fold in half, pull fold through end of row, pull ends through fold, pull tight.

Add fringe to end of each row on each short end of Scarf. ❑❑

Beige Scarf

SKILL LEVEL

INTERMEDIATE

FINISHED SIZE
3 x 54½ inches

MATERIALS
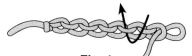
- ❏ Aunt Lydia's "Shimmer" Fashion fine (sport) weight thread (124 yds per ball): 2 balls #2242 light linen
- ❏ Size D/3/3.25mm crochet hook or size needed to obtain gauge

GAUGE
5 cross-sts = 2¼ inches; 9 rows = 3 inches

SPECIAL STITCH
Cross-stitch (cross-st): Sk next st, dc in next st, ch 1, working in back of last dc made, dc in st just sk.

INSTRUCTIONS

SCARF
Row 1: Ch 245, sc in **back bar** *(see Fig. 1)* of 2nd ch from hook and in back bar of each ch across, turn. *(244 sc)*

Fig. 1
Back Bar of Chain

Row 2: Ch 3, *(counts as first dc)*, [**cross-st** *(see Special Stitch)*] across, dc in last st, turn. *(121 cross-sts)*

Rows 3–8: Ch 3, [cross-st] across, dc in last st, turn.

Row 9: Sk all ch sps, ch 1, sc in each st across. Fasten off. ❏❏

Blue Scarf

FINISHED SIZE

3 x 67 inches

MATERIALS

❑ Red Heart LusterSheen fine (sport) weight yarn (4 oz/335 yds/113g per skein): 1 skein each #0995 ocean multi, #0824 medium blue and #0425 bluette
❑ Size D/3/3.25mm crochet hook or size needed to obtain gauge

GAUGE

5 dc = 1 inch; 10 rows = 3 inches

INSTRUCTIONS

SCARF

Row 1: With medium blue, ch 337, working in **back bar** (see Fig. 1) of chs, sc in 2nd ch from hook, hdc in next ch, dc in next ch, tr in next ch, dc in next ch, hdc in next ch, [sc in each of next 2 chs, hdc in next ch, dc in next ch, tr in next ch, dc in next ch, hdc in next ch] across to last ch, sc in last ch, turn. Fasten off. *(336 sts)*

Fig. 1
Back Bar of Chain

Row 2: Join ocean multi with sl st in first st, ch 4 *(counts as first tr)*, *dc in next st, hdc in next st, sc in next st, hdc in next st, dc in next st**, tr in each of next 2 sts, rep from * across, ending last rep at **, tr in last st, turn. Fasten off.

Row 3: Join ocean multi, with sl st in first st, ch 4, *dc in next st, hdc in next st, sc in next st, hdc in next st, dc in next st**, tr in each of next 2 sts, rep from * across, ending last rep at **, tr in last st, turn. Fasten off.

Row 4: Join medium blue with sc in first st, *hdc in next st, dc in next st, tr in next st, dc in next st, hdc in next st**, sc in each of next 2 sts, rep from * across, ending last rep at **, sc in last st, turn. Fasten off.

Row 5: Join bluette with sl st in first st, ch 1, dc in same st, dc in each st across, turn. Fasten off.

Row 6: Join medium blue with sc in first st, hdc in next st, dc in next st, tr in next st, dc in next st, hdc in next st, [sc in each of next 2 sts, hdc in next st, dc in next st, tr in next st, dc in next st, hdc in next st] across to last st, sc in last st, turn. Fasten off.

Rows 7 & 8: Rep rows 2 and 3.

Row 9: Join medium blue with sc in first st, *hdc in next st, dc in next st, tr in next st, dc in next st, hdc in next st**, sc in each of next 2 sts, rep from * across, ending last rep at **, sc in last st, turn. Fasten off.

Row 10: Working in ends of rows across short end, join medium blue with sc in first row, evenly sp 17 sc across ends of rows with 2 sc in end of row 9, sc in each st across with 2 sc in last st, evenly sp 18 sc across to end. Fasten off. ❑❑

Persimmon Scarf

SKILL LEVEL

INTERMEDIATE

FINISHED SIZE

2½ x 54¾ inches

MATERIALS

- ❑ Red Heart LusterSheen fine (sport) weight yarn (4 oz/335 yds/113g per skein): 1 skein each #0257 persimmon, #0332 tan and #0913 warm red
- ❑ Size D/3/3.25mm crochet hook or size needed to obtain gauge

GAUGE

6 sc = 1 inch; 5 rows = 1 inch

SPECIAL STITCH

V-stitch (V-st): (Dc, ch 1, dc) in next st.

INSTRUCTIONS

SCARF

Row 1: With tan, ch 324, sc in **back bar** *(see Fig. 1)* of 2nd ch from hook, sc in back bar of each ch across, turn. Fasten off. *(323 sc)*

Fig. 1
Back Bar of Chain

Row 2: Join red with sc in first st, [ch 1, sk next st, sc in next st] across, turn. Fasten off.

Row 3: Join tan with sc in first st, sc in each st and in each ch across, turn. Fasten off.

Row 4: Join persimmon with sl st in first st, ch 3, sk next st, **V-st** *(see Special Stitch)* in next st, [sk next 2 sts, V-st in next st] across to last 2 sts, sk next st, dc in last st, turn. *(2 dc, 107 V-sts)*

Row 5: Ch 4 *(counts as first dc and ch-1)*, [**dc dec** *(see Stitch Guide)* in next 2 sts, ch 2] across to last st, ch 1, dc in last st, turn. Fasten off.

Row 6: Rep row 3.

Row 7: Rep row 2.

Row 8: Rep row 3.

Rows 9 & 10: Rep rows 4 and 5. At end of last row, **do not turn**. Fasten off.

Row 11: Working in ends of rows, join tan with sc in end of row 3, evenly sp 11 sc across to row 10, 3 sc in first st, sc in each st and in each ch across with 3 sc in last st, working in ends of rows, evenly sp 11 sc across to row 3, sc in row 3, **do not turn**. Fasten off.

Row 12: Join red with sl st in end of row 2, working across sts on row 11, ch 1, sc in first st, ch 1, sk next st, [sc in next st, ch 1, sk next st] across with (sc, ch 1, sc) in each center corner st, sl st in end of row 2, **do not turn**. Fasten off.

Row 13: Join tan with sl st in end of row 1, working in sts across row 12, sc in each st and in each ch across with 2 sc in each corner ch sp, sl st in end of row 1. Fasten off. ❑❑

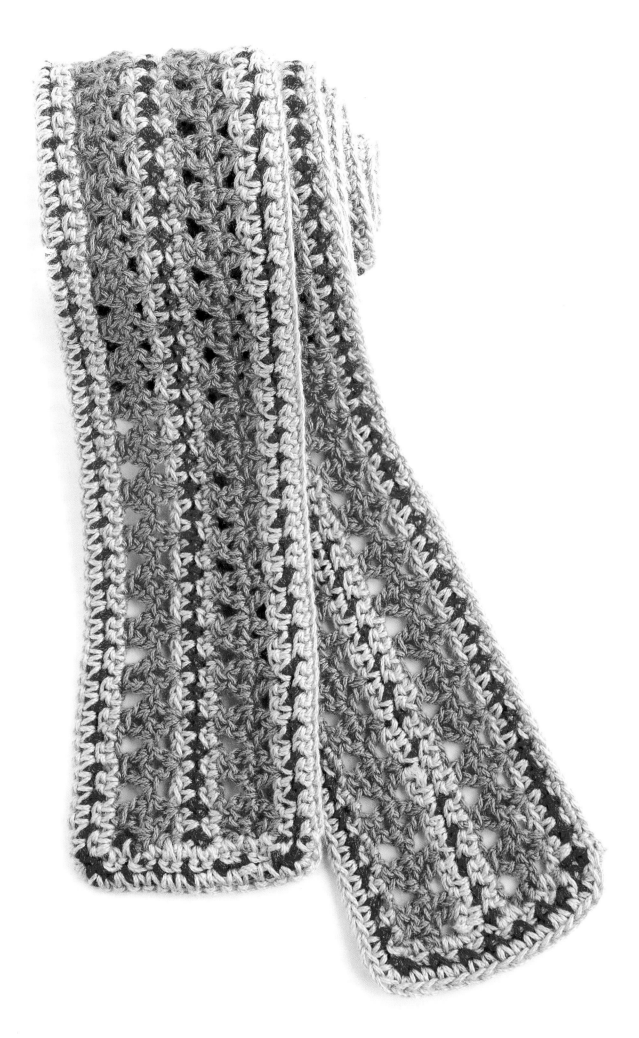

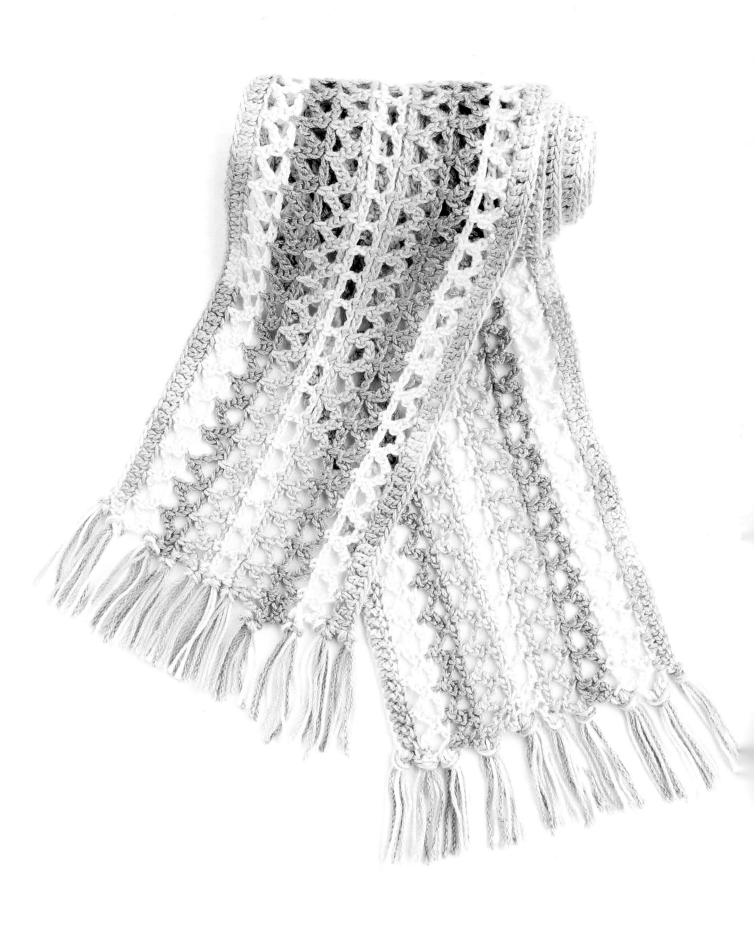

Multicolored Scarf

SKILL LEVEL

INTERMEDIATE

FINISHED SIZE

4¾ x 53 inches, excluding Fringe

MATERIALS

❏ Red Heart LusterSheen fine (sport) weight yarn (4 oz/335 yds/113g per skein): 1 skein each #0300 serenity multi, #0227 buttercup, #0425 bluette, #0246 peach and #0805 natural **FINE 2**
❏ Size D/3/3.25mm crochet hook or size needed to obtain gauge

GAUGE

23 dc = 4 inches; 8 rows = 2¼ inches

PATTERN NOTE

Leave 2-inch end at beginning and end of each row to be included in Fringe.

INSTRUCTIONS

SCARF

Row 1: With serenity multi (*see Pattern Note*), ch 309, dc in **back bar** (*see Fig. 1*) of 4th ch from hook (*first 2 chs count as first dc*) and in each ch across, turn. Fasten off. (*307 dc*)

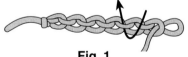

Fig. 1
Back Bar of Chain

Row 2: Join buttercup with sc in first st, [ch 5, sk next 2 sts, sc in next st] across, turn. Fasten off.

Row 3: Join buttercup with sc in 3rd ch of first ch-5 sp, [ch 2, sc in 3rd ch of next ch-5 sp] across, to last st, ch 1, dc in last st, turn. Fasten off.

Row 4: Join bluette with sc in first st, [ch 5, sk next ch sp, sc in next st] across, turn. Fasten off.

Row 5: Join bluette with sl st in first st, ch 4 (*counts as first dc and ch-1*), sc in 3rd ch of next ch-5 sp, [ch 2, sc in 3rd ch of next ch-5 sp] across to last st, ch 1, dc in last st, turn. Fasten off.

Row 6: Join peach with sc in first st, [ch 5, sk next ch sp, sc in next st] across, turn. Fasten off.

Row 7: Join peach with sl st in first st, ch 4, sc in 3rd ch of next ch-5 sp, [ch 2, sc in 3rd ch of next ch-5 sp] across to last st, ch 1, dc in last st, turn. Fasten off.

Row 8: Join natural with sc in first st, ch 1, sk next ch-1 sp, sc in next st, [ch 2, sk next ch sp, sc in next st] across to last st, ch 1, sc in last st, turn. Fasten off.

Row 9: Join natural with sl st in first st, ch 4, dc in next st, [ch 2, sk next ch sp, dc in next st] across to last st, ch 1, sk next ch sp, dc in last st, turn. Fasten off.

Row 10: Join peach with sc in first st, ch 1, sk next ch sp, sc in next st, [ch 2, sk next ch sp, sc in next st] across to last st, ch 1, sk next ch sp, sc in last st, turn. Fasten off.

Row 11: With peach, ch 3, join with sc in first st, [ch 5, sk next ch sp, sc in next st] across, ch 3, turn. Fasten off.

Row 12: Join bluette with sc in first ch of ch-3, ch 1, sc in 3rd ch of next ch-5 sp, [ch 2, sc in 3rd ch of next ch-5 sp] across, ending with ch 1, sc in last ch of ch-3, turn. Fasten off.

Row 13: Join bluette with sc in first st, [ch 5, sk next ch sp, sc in next st] across, turn. Fasten off.

Row 14: Join buttercup with sc in 3rd ch of first ch-5 sp, [ch 2, sc in 3rd ch of next ch-5 sp] across, turn. Fasten off.

Row 15: Join buttercup with sc in first st, [ch 5, sk next ch sp, sc in next st] across, ch 3, turn. Fasten off.

Row 16: Join serenity multi with sc in first ch of ch-3, ch 1, sc in 3rd ch of next ch-5 sp, [ch 2, sc in 3rd ch of next ch-5 sp] across, turn.

Row 17: Join serenity multi with sl st in first st, ch 1, dc in same st, dc in each st and in each ch across. Fasten off.

Fringe

Cut 1 strand of each color 4 inches in length. Holding all strands tog, fold in half, pull fold through, pull ends though fold. Pull to tighten.

Fringe in each end of rows 1, 2, 3, 5, 7, 9, 10, 12, 14, 16 and 17. ❏❏

Annie's Attic®

TOLL-FREE ORDER LINE or to request a free catalog (800) LV-ANNIE (800) 582-6643
Customer Service (800) AT-ANNIE (800) 282-6643, **Fax** (800) 882-6643
Visit AnniesAttic.com

We have made every effort to ensure the accuracy and completeness of these instructions. We cannot, however, be responsible for human error, typographical mistakes or variations in individual work.

ISBN: 978-1-59635-122-6

3 4 5 6 7 8 9

Stitch Guide

ABBREVIATIONS

beg	begin/beginning
bpdc	back post double crochet
bpsc	back post single crochet
bptr	back post treble crochet
CC	contrasting color
ch	chain stitch
ch-	refers to chain or space previously made (i.e., ch-1 space)
ch sp	chain space
cl	cluster
cm	centimeter(s)
dc	double crochet
dec	decrease/decreases/decreasing
dtr	double treble crochet
fpdc	front post double crochet
fpsc	front post single crochet
fptr	front post treble crochet
g	gram(s)
hdc	half double crochet
inc	increase/increases/increasing
lp(s)	loop(s)
MC	main color
mm	millimeter(s)
oz	ounce(s)
pc	popcorn
rem	remain/remaining
rep	repeat(s)
rnd(s)	round(s)
RS	right side
sc	single crochet
sk	skip(ped)
sl st	slip stitch
sp(s)	space(s)
st(s)	stitch(es)
tog	together
tr	treble crochet
trtr	triple treble
WS	wrong side
yd(s)	yard(s)
yo	yarn over

Chain—ch: Yo, pull through lp on hook.

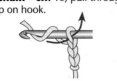

Slip stitch—sl st: Insert hook in st, yo, pull through both lps on hook.

Single crochet—sc: Insert hook in st, yo, pull through st, yo, pull through both lps on hook.

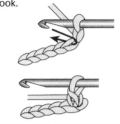

Front loop—front lp
Back loop—back lp

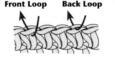

Front post stitch—fp:
Back post stitch—bp: When working post st, insert hook from right to left around post st on previous row.

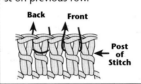

Half double crochet—hdc: Yo, insert hook in st, yo, pull through st, yo, pull through all 3 lps on hook.

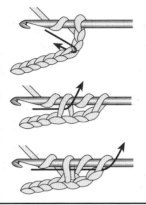

Double crochet—dc: Yo, insert hook in st, yo, pull through st, [yo, pull through 2 lps] twice.

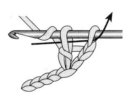

Change colors: Drop first color; with 2nd color, pull through last 2 lps of st.

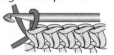

Treble crochet—tr: Yo 2 times, insert hook in st, yo, pull through st, [yo, pull through 2 lps] 3 times.

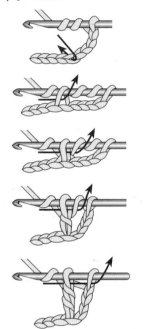

Double treble crochet—dtr: Yo 3 times, insert hook in st, yo, pull through st, [yo, pull through 2 lps] 4 times.

Single crochet decrease (sc dec): (Insert hook, yo, draw up a lp) in each of the sts indicated, yo, draw through all lps on hook.

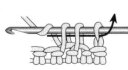

Example of 2-sc dec

Half double crochet decrease (hdc dec): (Yo, insert hook, yo, draw lp through) in each of the sts indicated, yo, draw through all lps on hook.

Example of 2-hdc dec

Double crochet decrease (dc dec): (Yo, insert hook, yo, draw lp through, yo, draw through 2 lps on hook) in each of the sts indicated, yo, draw through all lps on hook.

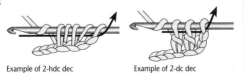

Example of 2-dc dec

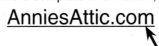

Example of 2-tr dec

Treble crochet decrease (tr dec): Holding back last lp of each st, tr in each of the sts indicated, yo, pull through all lps on hook.

US		UK
sl st (slip stitch)	=	sc (single crochet)
sc (single crochet)	=	dc (double crochet)
hdc (half double crochet)	=	htr (half treble crochet)
dc (double crochet)	=	tr (treble crochet)
tr (treble crochet)	=	dtr (double treble crochet)
dtr (double treble crochet)	=	ttr (triple treble crochet)
skip	=	miss

For more complete information, visit

AnniesAttic.com